Quinn   Stan St. Clair

Quinn

Quinn   Stan St. Clair

Cover design by Kent Grey-Hesselbein,
KGB Design Studio
Manchester, TN, USA
http://kghdesign.nvaazion.com/

If you enjoy this book, you may also like
these other books by Stan St. Clair

A Place in Time
(A historic novella about the American Reconstruction Era, the shutting down of the KKK, and the healing of the nation)
ISBN 978-0-9801704-8-1

Reflections on Life
(A collection of the nostalgic poetry of Stan St. Clair)
ISBN 978-0-9801704-1-2

A Proud Heritage:
the James Ansel Vinson Family Story
(The extended story of the Vinson family of this novella, with genealogy, limited edition)

Quinn

By Stan St. Clair

Based on a true story

Photographically illustrated

Edited by Michele Doucette

© 2009 by Stan St. Clair, St. Clair Publications

All rights reserved. No part of this publication may be reproduced or transmitted in any form by any means electronic or mechanical, including telecopy, recording, or any information storage and retrieval system now known or invented, without permission in writing from the publisher, except by a reviewer who wishes to quote brief passages in connection with a review written for inclusion in a magazine, newspaper or broadcast.

ISBN 978-0-9801704-7-4
Printed in the United States of America by
St. Clair Publications
P. O. Box 726
Mc Minnville, TN 37111-0726

http://stan.stclair.net

Quinn   Stan St. Clair

**In Honor of
James Lansing David Vinson
(3-26-1917 to 2-16-1936)**

Quinn   Stan St. Clair

This loving tribute to my special uncle is being released in commemoration of the 100th anniversary of the birth of my mother, Trula Vinson St. Clair, born August 6, 1909. She is sorely missed by many.

Stan

Table of Contents

Forward	9
Chapter One	10
Chapter Two	16
Chapter Three	22
Chapter Four	28
Chapter Five	36
Chapter Six	42
Chapter Seven	48
Chapter Eight	52
Chapter Nine	63
Chapter Ten	68
Chapter Eleven	76
Chapter Twelve	88

Chapter Thirteen	99
Chapter Fourteen	103

Photos

Trula and Wayne Baker, September, 1929	42
Trula's Graduation, May 1930	67
Trula with students in Wyoming, 1930-31	75
Trula and pony, Bartlett farm, Arkansas, 1934	86
Vinson kids "on the house", Scaly, NC, 1930's	87
Robert Wadlow and father, 1930's	98
The Vinson family, Scaly, NC, about 1936	102

Forward

This is the unique story of my uncle, "Quinn", whose brief span on earth passed before my time. It is partly woven from the wavering memories of my fading mother in years gone by; my uncles, Rowe and Atlas; and from thoughts passed down to others by my grandmother, Ethel Runion Vinson, and my first cousin once removed, Ednis Vest Foss. Special thanks go to my first cousin, Lonnie Vinson, who provided pertinent facts necessary for this story, and who, in fact, made its writing possible. A number of the details, and some incidents, have developed in wild imaginings of my mind. The majority of the characters are real people; the locales, correct.

His is a touching tale of triumph, compassion, and love, but one which ended too soon. Born into a struggling but warm family in the early 20th century, he was a mentally challenged, special person. The quandary which was to surround him would alter the destiny of his family, and all of their future generations.

Chapter One

"Oh God!" Ethel whispered, "What *am* I gonna do?"

Onward she pressed, deep into the forbidding storm. Fifteen cruel minutes seemed an hour. She was a mother, and must go forward. No other choice under heaven dared enter her mind. The temperature was plummeting at a dizzy pace.

Her husband, Ansel, was away to Sheridan, Wyoming for the final shopping trip, which he hoped would be completed before darkest winter's harsh arrival. His journeys from their homestead, near the tiny town of Kirby, Montana would last a full week with horse and buggy. Ethel had been whipping up a tantalizing pot of rabbit stew for the evening meal when she had become frightened by the sudden awareness that her special child was missing.

Earlier that cool, late October eve, two of her older children, Rowe and Trula had come bursting into the house like wild deer on a carefree summer morning. The two had been hiding to watch their "pet squirrel" in his final attempt to garner nuts before the impending rush of winter. Rowe had crashed ahead, with Trula, as usual, close at his heels. The heavy wooden door banged behind her, but a sudden gust kept it slightly ajar. Rowe dashed all the more swiftly, upward on the spiral staircase, to the warmth of the cozy loft. There, he gently plopped himself down near Eula and Dan, where they were napping on their pallets. Trula had paused to play Mama to baby Attie, who lay gurgling in a roughly hewn cradle by the flickering fire. Brother Quinn, still only five, recognized a glorious opportunity. He would explore the ever-forbidden. Out he dashed, tip-toeing to unlatch the gate leading from their yard into the vast forest.

"Sis", Ethel had said, her face stern and furrowed, "You're the oldest. That means you'll be in charge around here. Lansing's sneaked off. I've gotta go find him."

"But, Mama!"

"Don't you 'But Mama' me, young lady! You'll be just fine and dandy. Stay by the fire and take care o' Attie. If the others get up, just tell 'em I had to go out for a bit, and I'll be right back. You're a big girl, now, you're thirteen, for th' love o' Mike. You're practically a grown woman."

In a shocking flash, she was astraddle of her stunning white horse, Sonny, and had begun her frantic search. As always, she rode bareback, with only a blanket between her and the horse's active muscles. Streaks of icy snow soon whipped about her, as the bone-chilling edge of night came crashing around her.

The distant hooting of a great horned owl was smothered by the whistle of the quickening blizzard. Ethel could sense the terror of her predicament. Her nose had soon lost all feeling; her hands, though tightly wrapped in rags, were frozen to the reigns of the bridle. The lantern flickered in a futile flame. The horse was slowing. She clicked her tongue, gently tapping her heel on his side. Abruptly, in spite of her prodding, Sonny came to a dead standstill. Ethel hardly dared to glance downward. The haunting growl of a savage coyote was too close for comfort. Bolting her lantern upward, she could barely discern its snarling form.

"Gee!" she tugged the reign to the right, and edged away, skirting a huge pine. "Thank God", she whispered, more than relieved to have escaped the wily canine.

Her mind swirled as a funnel cloud upon the plains. She relived her wedding as a flash on the screen of her mind.

"Do you, James Ansel Vinson, take this, Ethel Melissa Runion, whom you hold by the right hand, to be your lawful and wedded wife? Do you promise to love, to honor, to cherish, to protect; forsaking all others, in sickness and in health, in adversity as well as prosperity; to cleave only unto her so long as you both shall live?"

"I do".

"Do you, Ethel Melissa Runion, take this, James Ansel Vinson, whom you hold by the right hand, to be your lawful and wedded husband..."

At that time her thoughts had flown to that propitious day in May, when the two of them had first locked glances. At that prolific moment, her heart had become as a pound of butter simmering in the heat of July. She had known without a glimmer of doubt, that no other man could ever fulfill Ansel's pre-destined mission in her life.

Finally, she had been gently nudged by her pending groom. "I do", she had mumbled, her eyes ablaze, "I certainly do!"

"Give him his reign," her mind wandered again, as she perceived Ansel's voice, as if at her side. He had once assured her that if she ever lost her way, a horse had a sense of direction. "Go, Sonny..." she paused, "go find Lansing."

Ethel jerked her head. Had she dosed? How much time had elapsed? Sonny was again stopped. Amazingly, she still clinched the lantern bale in her hand. The flame almost gone; she managed to turn up the wick. Sonny was moving slightly, whinnying and nudging an object on the ground. Ethel bolted from her mount. Gathering the figure in her arms, a silver tear trickled down her cheek, only to meet the freezing hand of Mother Nature. Sonny neighed loudly, his head nodding in joyous approval.

"Let's go home, Sonny!" Ethel said valiantly. And she gave him his reign once more.

Chapter Two

Ansel and J. Wilkins Vest had met while toiling in the copper mines of East Tennessee in '07 and '08. After cementing an enduring bond of friendship, Wilkins had taken Ansel home to meet his wife. The good news for Ansel had been the fact that Addie had a single sister. The wedding was November 8, 1908.

By '14, the Vests had ventured westward, in their eager search of the illusive American dream. In a flowery letter, the ambitious, avid pioneer, Wilkins, had urged the young couple to join his family on their grand quest for government land, and the certainty of a fabulous future. With spring's first comforting thaws, the Vinsons had joined them. The grueling eight-day journey from the Blue Ridge to the Rockies by locomotive had visibly shaken little Eula, who had experienced scathing nightmares. Older sister Trula's compassionate comforting had done little to soothe her torrid cries. Rowe was but a tiny tyke, but paid no mind to either of them.

In the following cycles of time, however, Ethel was to wonder if they had not been beckoned to the very pits of hell itself.

Most of eight years had elapsed, but not without incident. The Vinson homestead lay in a sprawling, fertile ravine in southeastern Montana, etched into the base of the picturesque Rosebud Mountains, in Big Horn County. This area was surely "God's country", if this trite expression might be used of any land, in any era. The homesteads lay just north of the Crow Reservation, established in 1904, near the site of Custer's infamous "Last Stand", and within a few miles of the land granted to the Northern Cheyenne. To their relief, by now, white man's relations were somewhat mended with the remnants of both tribes.

The Vinson place had been much improved from its original mass. Obtained as a square mile of virgin forest, it had first held a crude "dug-out", crested with a grass-thatched roof and bottomed with a hardened dirt floor. This fragile structure had soon given way to a comfortable wooden home, built by Ansel, a brave young adventurer; a carpenter by trade, and a freemason by choice.

The lazy curls of grey-blue smoke from the well-lain rock chimney trailed ever downward, as they encountered the dense humidity of the rapidly encroaching clouds. Barely over two months had gone by since they had been sadly informed of the death of their hero, William Frederick "Buffalo Bill" Cody'. An iconic Civil War soldier, and in later years, as a resident of Wyoming, he had become the eternal symbol of the Wild West. A part owner of the inn in Sheridan, he had even held auditions there for his shows, when in town. At his passing, tributes for him had come in from many prominent leaders, including King George and President Wilson.

Quinn had been born on a chilling morn, the twenty-sixth of March, in the year of our Lord nineteen hundred and seventeen. Ethel began her labor, and let out a guttural moan.

"Oh-h-h! Ansel, it's time, get the midwife".

"Are you sure, Love? Last time it took quite a spell."

"A-a-a-h! I said get the blessed midwife, Papa!'

Though no flakes were presently falling, a bulky white coat lay about the ravine as if to dare human challenge. Wrapping in his heaviest woolen garments, Ansel sped to the barn, as the wind beat savagely upon him. He tossed the scuffed English saddle over his chestnut stead, and buckled the belts as the horse danced about.

The ferocious wind forced icy branches to break, and tumble carelessly into his path. An hour escaped in barely seven miles.

"Hello! It's Vinson. Anybody here?" Not a sound. "Hello! Mrs. Marker" Frantic for help, he pounded the brown board door with an icy gloved fist. Finally, a painful moan from within made him cringe. With a sturdy post he forced the door inward, splintering the wooden latch and revealing the injured midwife sprawled in the floor, clutching a poker in her bleeding left hand.

"Are you O.K.?" Ansel said, scooping her up in his brawny arms.

"I tripped over my little Lillie!"

"Lillie?"

"My dog!" she said, with an eerie screech. "I think my leg's broken."

"Do you have any liquor in the house?"

"A bit of whiskey I use for toddies It's in the cabinet directly behind the stove."

Soon he had administered a healthy dose, and constructed a splint from small sticks wrapped with strips of a sheet. Carefully mounting her on the stallion behind the saddle, he wound through the woods, toward home.

"It's a boy!" Mrs. Marker cried. "Thank God, we got here in time."

"His name is James Lansing David", Ansel said.

"Where'd ya come up with that one?"

"Well, my first name is James, though, as you know, I don't go by it. My dad was David, and we're using city names. Lansing is in Michigan."

"'Tis a whale of a handle for such a wee one."

But his family called him simply, "Quinn", or Lansing when speaking to others.

Within Lansing's first year, it became sadly apparent that he would develop at a slower pace than the previous three, and must be guarded closely, as a rule, by his siblings.

Chapter Three

The village of Kirby was nestled snugly at the base of the mountains. The gelid creek which rambled through the rich green valley gave freshness to life, as the seasons rose and fell. Snow was constantly visible on the scenic peaks, and came plummeting from the heavens, at least to some slight extent, most years, in all months but July.

The farming season following the incident with Quinn had yielded a meager supply. A summer plague of pesky grasshoppers had taken a great toll on the crops. Winter's wrath, paying no attention to the scarcity of food, swept through the valley with all the fury of a diabolical plot. The Vinson ravine was soon enveloped in multiple blankets of driven ice. Chords of firewood had been chopped and split in anticipation of a long, hard winter.

There were so few of the vegetables and berries which Ethel had managed to can, that they quickly diminished. The one remaining hope lay in the oatmeal which had been a staple at their breakfast table. Ethel knew that it must be used sparingly. Watered down, it had become their solitary source of nourishment.

It was early on a late December morn, and. the children were still sleeping in the loft. As Ansel's manly voice broke the somber stillness, Ethel plunged for the kitchen wall. Sinking to the floor, her breath released in painful moans.

"Love! What's the matter?"

"The room's spinning, help me lay down."

Luckily, the doctor was home. The breeze had fallen silent, but the sun was on extended vacation. The grey of the welkin above seemed a dreary harbinger of the harshness of the balance of the season, yet to completely unravel. The snow had been shoveled from the fore of the house, and the horse's hooves had beaten a hardened path to Kirby.

"She'll need a lot of rest, but the best thing you can do for her is to get her some meat broth."

"But where are we going to get meat. Even the small animals seem to have gone away in search of food this year." *except...* Ansel thought.

"Tomatoes", Ethel said. "I crave tomatoes!"

"But we've got none of those either, you know all we have is oatmeal," then turning to Trula, he said, "Go to Kirby, Sis, and ask at all the stores till somebody will let you have some tomatoes on credit."

Young Trula trudged the seven miles into town, playing games by blowing rings of steam with her breath. Once, she lay on the solid white surface beside the road and forced a shallow snow angel.

"Mr. George, my mama needs some tomatoes, she's sick, Papa said to ask you if we could get some on credit."

Quinn

"Get on home girl; you know we can't give credit here. Nobody's gonna be able to wait on the money till next fall!"

And so it went, once again. Trula was in tears, and blowing on her bare hands, hoping to turn the blue back to a flesh tone. At last, she entered the third and final store. There was Wilkins Vest, at the counter, laying down a few coins to fill a paltry order.

"Hey, gal! Why the tears?"

"Oh, Uncle Wilkins! Mama's bad sick!" Gushes of silvery liquid streamed down her cheeks. "She needs some tomatoes somethin' fierce! And the doctor said she needs broth, too!"

Wilkins choked. He was a man. He couldn't afford to let his ducts secrete the warm moisture which was aching to come forth.

"Now, Trula, Deary, we'll do something", Then, staring into the storekeeper's eyes, the two agreed, without a word. The tomatoes were in Trula's hands. Two cans of them.

"I don't have any broth. I hope this will help your Ma."

"Don't worry," said Wilkins, "I'll see that you get your money."

Meanwhile, at the homestead, another scenario had played out. When Ansel had crept from the house with his .22 rifle, the other children had been spellbound by a game of checkers in which Rowe and Eula had been engaged. But Quinn had peeped curiously, as was his intrinsic nature, through the frosty pane, his eyes ever upon his papa. When the crack of the rifle had sounded, it had startled them all.

Trula came dashing in with a grin, half frozen, handing the tomatoes proudly to her papa. The savory smell of wild meat boiling on a pot over the open fireplace wafted through the room. "Oh, goody! You got some meat for Mama to have broth! Where'd you get it?"

"The Lord has provided," Ansel said calmly.

"But where did you *get* it?" Trula bolted once more for the door. She had to see... just had to know. But her pet squirrel would not answer her call.

Chapter Four

"Sis! There's somebody at the door. Can you get it? I'm dippin' these beans into the mason jars."

"Sure, Mama. Why, hello, Eva, come on in!"

Eva Ghostbull was growing into a beauteous young lady.

It had been during the Vinsons' second spring at the homestead that the Ghostbull family had drifted into their lives.

In a morning fog, while hunting, Ansel had bumped into a shabby lean-to near the border of the Reservation of Northern Cheyenne. A 12 gage shotgun was pointed squarely at his nose. Hands skyward, he had edged forward. "I wish you no harm, neighbor. My pup, Amos, is on the trail of a rabbit. Name's Vinson. I live about five miles southwest of here on Rosebud Creek."

"Ghostbull, Arthur Ghostbull. We have a right here, Mister. Your government's given us a patent, if we can trust 'em. It was all our land till the dern white man stole it! We wanta be peaceable. We want no trouble with you settlers."

"Didn't think you did, neighbor. I just want the same."

The swarthy native had grunted, and eased the gun to his side. The warming breeze had whipped a platted raven braid over his left shoulder. Dressed in the common denim of his visitor, and a coat made of furs, Ghostbull resented the loss of his heritage.

"We call this breeze a Chinook."

"Why's that?"

"There's a legend among our people that Chinook, uh, you white men would say, uh, 'snow-eater', was the name of a pretty young squaw who disappeared with no warning while walking in the woods in the springtime.

Many braves search for her for many moons, but not find her. While some still looked for her, a warm breeze was sent down from the mountains by the Great Spirit. It moved across our land. This brought the summer close behind. That's why we call the breeze 'Chinook'."

"That's a beautiful story. Thank you for sharing with me."

"Want a smoke?"

"Have one of mine?" Ansel had answered in a calm tone.

As they had enjoyed a few puffs of home-grown tobacco, Ansel had continued. "I've got a touch of red blood in me, too."

"Ugh! Ya don't say?"

"My papa's mama was part Cherokee. They drove her people out of our country about fifty years before I was born. My grandma's family hid in the woods. Most of the rest of 'em were marched to Oklahoma Territory. Lots of 'em died. I know the meaning of shame over th' actions of our people. I get hoppin' mad every time I think about it."

"Then I guess we not be so different, after all."

The two had parted as new friends after Arthur had introduced him to his wife, Sarah. Each had granted the other a gift. Ansel had given Arthur a pouch of smoking tobacco; Arthur had handed him some hides which he could trade for salt, sugar and other staples.

When the Ghostbulls had first come calling in their wagon, a tiny round head had peeked from behind Sarah's skirt.

"Eva," Ethel had said, this is Trula. "We call her 'Sis'. She's your age." Eula had stood at a distance, a crease in her brow, while Rowe had walked away, and pretended to have not the slightest care.

"Wanta play with my china doll?" Trula had asked.

"Sure!"

"Ansel", Arthur had said, "I hear from others that you are a builder. They say you built Post Office in Kirby."

"Folks do talk, now don't they? I do my best."

"Sarah and I need a house built. You saw where we're livin'. We stay a lot in our wagon. I've got a little money saved from my hides and the sale o' my ponies and chickens. I'll pay as you go, money, and whatever I have your family can use. And I have lumber I traded for."

"That's fine by me, friend. I'll start on Monday."

"How do you make your soap, Ethel", Sarah had asked.

"It's called lye soap. It comes from the tallow of animals that I rendered with ashes. I'll give you some when you go."

A fine little home soon graced the land of his Indian friends, and their families were drawn closer in the process.

That first day that Trula had met her best friend, now seemed to have been an eternity ago. Over seven years had come and gone. Both girls were now nearing their fifteenth birthdays.

Quinn was feeding a chipmunk which had climbed up his leg, and had come to rest upon his head.

"They're starting a school in Kirby, Eva. Papa's been teaching us older kids at home, you know, but now we get to go to a real school!"

"I wonder what that will be like."

"I don't know, but I bet it'll be great!"

"Hey! You haven't seen my baby sister! Her name's Elsie. Wantta see her?"

"M-my baby!" Quinn squealed. "My Essie!"

"Now, Quinn, settle down and hold my hand. I'll take you and Eva in to see her."

"O. K., Sis, O.K."

"I don't like it here. Can't we go home, Sis?"

"No, Eula. We have to get educated. That's gonna make us smart kids, so we can be good workers, and folks will respect us. And Papa says we'll be wives and mommies some day, and we need to know lots of stuff to do that."

"Yuck! I just want to go back home to Mama. She can teach me what I need to know."

"Be good, Eula." Rowe frowned.

"My name is Rose Smith. I'll be the teacher this summer. As you kids know, we can only have classes for three months because of the weather, and we don't have enough children around to get a bigger building. James Hardwick donated this house to use, so it will be known as the Hardwick School. Any questions?"

Rowe was reminiscing about his chilling experience, at age six. He had been asked to recite a poem at a gathering of farmers. It had scared him to death, but he had done an excellent job. After a few moments of silence, when it was apparent that no one else was going to speak, he said, "Yeah, Miss Smith, when is recess?"

Chapter Five

"It's snowing hard! Let's go home!" Eula whined, "I'm cold!" The dog was at her side.

"I have to admit, heavy snow in August is a tough break. But you know Papa will whip us if we don't go on to school!" Trula had the resolve of a mother. "Let's play a game, Rowe. We'll make believe that the snow is a blanket. And we'll play *I Spy*!"

"I don't feel like it!" Eula blurted.

"Sis's right," Rowe said, "I spy somethin'... blue".

"Well it sure ain't the stupid sky!" Eula said, with a frown. "See, there's the school, nobody's there!"

Amos barked heartily, as if to agree.

Eula's tears gushed as they trudged homeward.

"Hey, Uncle Harley, I see you've got some wood chopped!" Rowe said.

"Yep! Choppin' wood keeps me from freezin' in weather like this, and builds my muscles to boot! I see you kids made it back OK. No school today, ha, ha! Get yourselves inside and warm up."

"I'm glad you came up here, Uncle Harley. You're a lot of help to us," Trula said.

"Br-r-r-!" Rowe kicked the snow from his boots, but Eula ran on in, taking the icy white flakes with her.

"Get back out here and clean your shoes, Eula!" Trula said.

"Oh, Sis, you ain't my mama!'

"No, she's not, but I am, and if you don't want your fanny swatted, do what your sister told you!"

"Coffeen School was a help; a bit better than Hardwick. At least you kids got in a couple more grades, but you're still behind. I've found you and Sis a way to catch up on your schooling," Ansel told Rowe. The years had seemed to fly. "You will be staying with a nice family where I helped build their home. It's the finest house in Kirby. You'll be right near the school."

"Who are they?" Trula said, overhearing from the kitchen, where she had been helping her mother cook supper.

"They're the Johnsons. Do you remember Mama and me talking about the Spear family who own the cattle yard and the dry good store in Sheridan? Well, Mrs. Johnson is their daughter. They're well-to-do, and you both must be on your best manners at all times."

"How can you pay for it, Papa?"

"I'm trading them pork for your board."

Quinn squinted. His voice was quiet. "Can I go, too, Papa?"

"No, Son. You are our special boy. Mama and I can't do without you for even <u>one day</u>!"

Quinn grinned. "O-oh, Papa, th-thank you. I-I love you!"

"Thanks for letting me ride the pony to school, Mrs. Johnson." Trula reached to hug her, but her hostess resisted.

This house is my castle, Trula's thought flooded her being, as she stood atop the classy knotty maple staircase which her father had built. It was Saturday night. In the lavish parlor below, a fabulous ball was in progress. The dim light of the stairs faded her presence from view. She saw herself below, as surely as if it were happening - the dashing belle of the ball, being swept away by a stunning young nobleman.

But then, there came stark reality. She must wash the dishes for all of the boarders to help pay her way.

"Who was at the door, Ansel?"

"It was the truant officers, again, Love. They say we have to get the children into full time school. We'll have to move somewhere we can get a good education for all these younguns. We've got so many that they won't ignore it any more. As good a place as we have here, we can't afford to board all the kids in town, and we can't teach 'em all they need to know. A brand new world is blooming around us."

"Where will we go? Wilkins and Addie want us to stay around here."

"I talked to Harley the other day. I told him it might come to this. He says he'll give up his homestead and move with us. I don't know about Wilkins and Addie. But they've got their kids to get educated, too. Will Furman says he'll take over the homestead.

"He doesn't have much to offer us, but it'll satisfy the government's requirements, and it won't go back to them."

"Whatever you say, Ansel. As long as we all have each other, we'll be fine."

"We'll go down around Sheridan. I've met some nice folks there."

Ethel's warm eyes smiled. For her, their love was enough to weather life's endless storms.

Trula with Wayne Baker, September, 1929

Chapter Six

"Come on out, Ruel! The creek's safe."

Prairie Dog Creek was frozen solid. Winter was quickly marching in. Rowe had traded a large pouch of marbles for a used, but sparkling, pair of ice skates. He felt heavenly as he glided about on the wide expanse of the creek.

His cousins, Ruel Vest, and his sisters, Leona, Geneva, and Ednis were visiting from nearby Montana,

"I don't know. I don't have any skates. What if I fall through?"

Rowe's laugh made him even more nervous. "Come on, man. I'll help you if you fall down."

"Leona, will you go with me?"

"Na, call me chicken if you want. I'm staying here with Trula. Monroe will come out"

"OK," Monroe Ferris said. "I'm game." Monroe skated sans skates without a problem. He was a neighbor like Wayne Baker. Monroe enjoyed spending time with Rowe, while Wayne had a different motive for hanging around. His pleasant thoughts of Trula were quite honorable. He would use the animals on the farm as an excuse to be there. He was especially fond of feeding the stubborn mules and frisky horses. Trula showed friendship, but cared not a whit for anything more.

"Whee!' Ruel said, as his feet went flying out from under him.

Rowe gently glided up, carefully lifting his cousin to his feet. "You're alright. You've just gotta get the hang of it. I got out here and slid around a lot before I got skates.

Ruel smiled, but groaned. Yes, he would get the hang of it, alright. But he didn't want to kill himself in the process. To relieve his mind, he thought of how good one of Aunt Ethel's pumpkin pies would taste about then.

Quinn just stood back and laughed. "I-I ain't goin' out there! N-no sir re bob-tail Johnson!"

Trula smiled and looked at Leona. "That's my boy! Aren't you the smart one, now!"

Before buying the one-hundred-acre ranch at M.K., which bordered on scenic Prairie Dog Creek at its intersection with the rushing Tongue River, the families of Ansel and Harley had made their home in the town of Sheridan. Ansel had found employment with the C. B. and Q. Railroad, and worked part time with the Burlington shops there.

Harley had gone home and married; then he and Bessie had brought two children into the world while in the West. Both had died. After the trauma which this tragedy brought, they had returned to their native North Carolina mountains.

Another reason for Ansel's purchasing the place at M.K., about seventeen miles northeast of town, was the fact that it encircled a one-room school building, originally constructed by a man named Ed Harris, and his friends, on land donated by the Evans family. Classes were already in progress.

"What's wrong, Eula, you can hardly talk." Sis said one day in early December, 1925.

"My throat hurts real bad." Eula strained to speak weakly.

"I'll fix you some salt water."

But her condition failed to improve.

"She has septic sore throat," The doctor said. "Just rub her forehead with damp cloths, and make her gargle the salt water every few hours."

Preacher Blacklodge offered prayers on her behalf, but her healing was not to be.

"Dear friends, we are gathered here this day to commit this precious young lass into God's hands. She has shed the bonds of this mortal clay, and gone on to be with Him. Jesus said, 'Suffer the little children to come unto me, and forbid them not: for of such is the kingdom of God.' Let us pray, Dear Heavenly Father, giver and taker of life, comfort this fine family, and let them know that some day they will join their loved one in heaven with you, in the name of your precious Son, amen."

It was ten days before Christmas, and only twelve days before her fourteenth birthday. That morning, when they arose, their dear Eula had been gone.

Deep pangs had pierced Ethel's heart, as a dull knife, ripping the very life from her. Ansel had fallen to his knees. Trula and Rowe had cried at her bedside.

She was laid to rest on the hillside above the school.

Though nothing could bring her back, another would soon come along to help ease their pain. Just over four months later, Jesse was born. His middle name was Salem, a city name meaning peace.

Chapter Seven

"Shane, W. A. Shane"

"Nice to meet you, Shane"

"I'm the Indian agent for Sheridan County. I'm also in charge of preservation of the buffalo."

"Somebody sure needs to be in charge," Ansel said. "There's less and less of 'em around. And I'm glad to have met the agent for the Indians. We aren't having any problems with them. You must be doing a good job."

"I try."

"Won't you join us for dinner? Ethel's cooking up some good grub."

"Now a man don't need to be turnin' down good victuals! Don't mind if I do, if you really mean it."

"Miss Ethel, you are *some* cook! That's the finest polk salad and fried Irish taters I've had in quite a spell! And m-m-m, m-m-m! What fantastic fried chicken!"

"Why, thank you, Mr. Shane! You're quite the gentleman!" She glanced at Ansel as if to say, *why can't you say stuff like that?*

After several pleasant visits, W.A. Shane became a regular at the Vinson home. Often he would take Quinn on his knee after an evening meal, and whisk him away in yarns of fantastic proportion, while Rowe and Dan sat by, spellbound in the magic which their new friend had woven.

"Hey, Little Man!" he said, twisting the end of his mustache with his right thumb and forefinger, "I really appreciate you lettin' me hold you on my knee and tell you my adventures. What say you folks let him come with me to meet some of my Cheyenne friends who are working here?"

"I don't know... we don't let Lansing away without one of us..." Ethel paused. "He's a very special little fellow, you know! And he's just nine."

"Take me, too," Rowe said, reflecting a tone of urgency. "We had some Cheyenne friends in Montana at th' reservation."

"How about it, folks? I'll take 'em both tomorrow mornin', and have 'em back in time for supper."

"Now you boys behave, and mind Mr. Shane," Ansel said, as he tucked in Quinn's flannel shirt. "If he has to spank either of you, you'll get a second helpin' when you get home!"

"We'll be good, Papa, I promise! An' I'll help Mr. Shane with Lansing."

As the trio arrived at the home near Sheridan, a brawl was brewing. Two young braves were in a heated discussion.

"AAahovêê.stse!" One said. Then spotting Shane, he addressed the agent, "EEohkêêsááa'-ááahtomóónééhe."

"Ováa'na'xaeotse!" Shane said firmly. You must work this out. To get angry will only make him not listen to you all the more."

Soon, Shane had achieved peace between the braves. Rowe shook his head in amazement. "What were they saying?"

"The one who spoke first said that his brother was not listening to him. I told him to calm down. When one works out his problems with angry words, no good will come of it. The Great Spirit works to bring peace."

Quinn was smiling broadly. "Y-you did a good thing, M-mister Shane."

"Thanks, son!"

"Look!" Rowe said, "it's Amos! He followed us!" The husky black-and-white family canine was showing his teeth, in a friendly sort of way. Wagging his tail briskly, he crept nearer to Rowe.

That night at the M.K. ranch, the boys told Ansel how Shane had handled the argument between the two Indian brothers.

"You're a fine example to my young sons, Shane. I would like for you to join us for church services this Sunday."

"I never was much for public worship. My church is on the open range. Nature shows forth the workings of the Great Spirit. We must protect the elements and the wildlife. The bison are disappearing from our hills. Much of our forest is falling because of the coming of the white man. I identify with the people I protect."

"I understand, my brother, but we find God helps us when we ask him to work in our hearts."

That Sunday the Vinson children were baptized. As they trekked toward home, Rowe said to Trula, "I don't feel any different."

"Me either."

Quinn   Stan St. Clair

From behind a mighty oak, Shane's lips curled upward on one side.

Chapter Eight

"Rowe, go feed the cows."

"Sure, Papa."

A Chinook blew in, signaling the primal spring thaw. The still-blanched pasture lay on the opposite bank of the mighty Tongue River. The usual route took a bit of time, as it required trailing along Prairie Dog Creek to a low point near its mouth.

I'll take a short cut, Rowe thought. Across the icy river he dauntlessly ventured. But Quinn was watching his every move. Nearing the far side, a sudden crackling beneath his feet brought Rowe's mind to a whirr. The cruel river was pulling him rapidly under! Quinn let out a quickened scream, bringing his father bolting from the house. Plunging for the bank, he was able to snatch the bare root of a tree.

"Hold on, Son! I'm coming!"

Quinn   Stan St. Clair

The frigid force of the raging Tongue slashed his legs against the ice beneath the surface.

Ansel dashed to the ford. The laughing river was savagely sliding Rowe's hands from the root.

"I'm coming, Rowe! Just hold tight! For heaven's sake, don't give up!"

But the root was slipping away, and Rowe's freezing hands turning purple. Suddenly, the root was gone. Rowe could feel his body sinking under! At his side, Ansel dove for him, grabbing his frightened son by one arm. Like a great vacuum cleaner, the river sucked them onward, and into the force of the current, breaking the thin ice in its path. With his free hand, Ansel fought the twin forces of nature and time. Grasping a huge block of ice, and pulling upward, he used it as a raft.

With a solid bang, they had encountered a solid mass: a tree which had submerged beneath the surface in a storm during the winter! Following its trunk to the base of its roots at the bank, the two were released to freedom.

"Hot cocoa never tasted so grand! God protected you, Son!"

"With a little help from you!"

"Y-yeah! And me. D-don't forget me!" Quinn chimed in.

As the thaws progressed, the school year wound down. Trula was now boarding with the Stone Family, attending high school in Sheridan, and home on weekends.

"When you get out, I want you to study to be a doctor, Sis. You can do anything you want; all you have to do is set your mind to it!"

"Oh, Papa! I don't want to be a doctor! All I want to do is teach school. There are lots of kids around here that need a good teacher."

"Like I said, Sis, you can do anything you want badly enough. But the folks around here need a good doctor, too."

"I've got something I want to do, too"

"What's that, Papa?"

"I want to have a corn mill like your grandpa Vinson has back home. Nobody else has one around here."

"But, Papa! How are you gonna do that?"

"I'm going to build one. I'll figure a way for the Dodge to run it."

Rounding a two-by-four on all corners, he jacked the car up, and bolted it into place. Attaching a pulley to the two-by-four, he devised a way to bring it into position under the touring car, and his mill was operative.

"Hey, Sam, how in the world are you, man? I've got my corn mill running, and you make the flour in your mill. Why don't we swap out?"

"Sounds fine to me. Help yourself, and give me twenty-five pounds of meal."

"By the way, what would you take for that old Packard of yours?"

Ansel had been eyeing the twelve cylinder tank-of-a-car for some time.

"Aw, I don't know, Vinson. What would ya give me?"

"Now, Weltner, it's a gas hog, and you know it. Can't be worth much with money so hard to come by, and gas in short supply. How about fifty dollars?"

"I'll take seventy-five."

"I'll go sixty, and not a red cent more."

"You just bought yourself a classic, Vinson!"

The Packard still looked great, and ran like new. All the kids loved it, and Quinn squealed to go for a ride every day.

"Pardon me, sir, but you look familiar."

"Hemingway. Ernest."

"Mr. Hemingway! I'm a big fan of your work! I am going to be a teacher when I graduate from Sheridan High. I can't believe I met you at a library. Imagine you, here in Sheridan! What brings you to our town?"

"I'm starting a new novel about the Great War. I won't spoil the plot for you, but it's to be titled, 'A Farewell to Arms'."

"Are you staying here?"

"Yes, I'm at the Sheridan Inn. The one with which our friend, Bill Cody, was affiliated here."

"I might have known. I will await with great anticipation the publication of your book, Mr. Hemmingway!"

"Ernest, please. You didn't even tell me, what is your name, young lady?"

"Trula Vinson. My dad's a rancher."

"It's good to meet such a fine young lady who's interested in the education of our next generation."

"My, Mr., uh, Ernest, the pleasure is all mine!"

"I must be getting back to the inn. I hope you the best, young Trula. Good day!"

"Whee! Last one in is a chicken! Cluck, cluck, cluck!" Monroe Ferris said, one hot August afternoon.

During the summer the rambunctious Vinson boys would delight in jumping from an overhanging limb into the deepest stretch of Prairie Dog Creek. As the boys swam, they watched the colorful sparrows flitting about their nests in a wall of rock near the bank.

"Rowe, Monroe, I've got a project for you boys. You've got nothing better to do than swim, and laugh and bird-watch, and the like. Put your energy to work and build your muscles. We can dam up this creek and channel it into a centrifugal pump I've got. I'll hook it up to a six-horsepower gasoline engine, which I also just happen to have, by the way", Ansel was smiling. "We'll dig ditches in the fields, and force it into 'em. This will irrigate our crops."

Ansel's plan worked like a charm until it reached the gopher network.

"Rowe," he said, "get some corn stalks and stop up those stinkin' gopher holes!"

"Let Dan help. He's sittin' here not doin' a dad-blamed thing!"

"Who did I ask? Dan's just a little kid"

"Me."

"Then get to work!" But when he turned toward him, Rowe had disappeared.

Chapter Nine

"Get up, Dan!"

"I don't know why ya'll named that horse Dan!"

"He reminds me so much o' my brother! Ha! Na-a-w, you know that, Mama! Johnny Trembath named him that before we got 'im!" Rowe gently tapped the sleek sorrel stallion on the buttock with his open hand, and Dan galloped freely about the yard. Coming to a halt, Rowe dismounted and headed toward the well for a cooling dipper of water. The great leather reigns plopped to the ground. Elsie quickly wound them casually about her tiny body.

"Here, catch!" Two-year-old Jesse tossed a wood chip high into the air, striking the horse on the flank with shocking impact!

The startled stallion neighed, and lunged forward. The frightened Elsie bounced across the clods, and through the prickly beds of tiny cactus in his path!

Rowe frantically darted for the house and grabbed a 30-30. He aimed carefully for the horse's head, his finger nervously clinching the trigger. At that pivotal moment, the panic-stricken child was loosed. The horse, of course, never knew how lucky he had been.

"What in tarnation's going on?" Rowe said to Atlas one summer's day in 1929. Attie's face was a pale ashen hue, and he was vomiting.

"I was takin' a walk with Lansing down by the gully and..."

"Not the big gully Papa warned us to stay away from!"

"Yeah, that gully."

"Oh, no! What happened?"

"There was a dead buffalo in there, and some Crow Indians were cuttin' off meat They must be awfully hungry."

"We need to let Mr. Shane know. Maybe he can help 'em."

Quinn was hanging on their every word. "I-I'll tell him. Please let me?"

"Sure, Quinn. You're his buddy." Atlas said; a tad of sarcasm in his voice.

"That bison was poisoned by farmers who were trying to keep the coyotes away. I was told so by one of them," Shane said. "Thanks, Quinn; you, too, Attie and Rowe. We've gotta warn the Crow, *and* the Cheyenne. We could have an epidemic of food poisoning."

For the next several days, Shane spread the word about the entire area. He also used his authority to have the marshal force the farmers to bury the carcass of the decaying bison. Quinn was commended by the local sheriff's office. But the commendation was not appreciated by the farmers.

Trula's Graduation, May, 1930
Sheridan, Wyoming

Chapter Ten

"That crazy Vinson boy's stirred up trouble for us."

"What're we gonna do about it? That's not the only thing he's done. He hit my boy the other day at the store. He can't learn. He's an embarrassment, that's what he is! His parents need to keep him at home."

The gossip at the street-side checker games and the buzzing barber shop in Sheridan reflected animosity and disdain over Quinn more than ever. Neighbor children began to mimic him to his siblings.

"Lansing's a d-dummy! That crazy brother o' yours ought to be put in a n-nut house!"

"He's not crazy!" Dan stormed. "He's my brother!" Dan dashed angrily home from school, bathing his face in tears.

"What should we do, Papa?" Ethel asked.

Quinn   Stan St. Clair

"Just watch him carefully. He doesn't mean any harm. He's a good kid. He's never done anything to hurt anyone intentionally."

"The Oltz's will help us. Since they don't have any kids, they've taken a shine to him, about like Shane."

In spite of their most concerted efforts to shelter Quinn from the growing sneers of other children, and the pangs of prejudice in the small clandestine community, one fall day in 1930, a brisk knock came at their door, which was to become the forerunner of unfortunate fate.

"Mrs. Vinson, we've had a complaint from one of your neighbors. They say you have a retarded boy, called Lansing, that's caused some problems."

"Sir," Ethel said sternly, "our boy doesn't hurt anybody. And we keep him inside, what time Mrs. Oltz doesn't have him. My husband drives him over to stay with them some days, when we're going to town, or need to be away for a bit."

"But where was he Thursday afternoon?" the sheriff asked. "A man told my office that he was bothering his little girl."

"What do you mean, *bothering*? My boy's only thirteen, and as you know, he's slow."

"The man said he was talking to her when his car broke down on the road between here and Decker. He doesn't want your boy anywhere around his girl."

"Talking to her, huh? Is that a crime? Yes, he was at the Oltz's on Thursday, and that's up close to Decker. We love our son and he's a good boy."

"I ain't doubtin' that, ma'am."

"What do you want us to do?"

"This man has made a complaint to the state. You'll be hearin' from them directly, I reckon.

Good day, Mrs. Vinson" The sheriff tipped his hat. Ethel cried.

Trula had graduated from Sheridan High. In her final year she had earned her certificate in Normal Training. This term she was staying away, teaching a school at Spring Willow, in the Plumb Creek District. She had five students ranging in age from eight to fifteen. On weekends, Rowe would drive his 1925 Star to pick her up and carry her home. One day he took along his chum, Happy Bealan.

"Sis, this is Happy. He lives with Johnny Trembath."

"Happy, huh? What's he so happy about?"

"That's his nickname. He laughs a lot. I wanted you to meet 'im."

"Hi Happy, I'm Trula."

"Yeah, I know," a giggle separated his words. "Rowe's told me all about you. You're that smart teacher sister of his."

"Is that what he told you?"

"Sure thing. He says you stay by yourself down here at this school all week. You must be kinda lonesome down here, huh? You like boys?"

"I like ones who don't talk so much, and mind their manners. I had to teach some boys a lesson today. They thought it was funny to throw snow balls in the classroom while I was grading papers after school yesterday. They thought I didn't see them as they left. They got a switching today."

"Wow! I guess I gotta watch it around you!"

Next time, Happy didn't come.

Rowe had grown close to an elderly couple named Beaumont. Both of them were uncommonly attached to him. He was quite handy on their ranch, and could handle their toughest chores.

Quinn   Stan St. Clair

Ansel would make his rounds in Sheridan, truck farming out of his huge Lincoln automobile, which had replaced the Packard. Together, the two of them brought in the needed funds in the early days of the Great Depression.

Within a short fortnight of the sheriff's visit, the state officer came calling.

"Mr. and Mrs. Vinson," he said, "We've got no choice. The state of Wyoming requires that all handicapped youth be institutionalized. You'll be allowed to visit on specified weekends, after he's had a chance to settle in. The home is at Lander, the other side of the Big Horns. Here's the address."

Without their special son, the family felt a darkened corner, a void which no one else could satisfy. Each allotted visit held a mixture of emotions. The anticipation of the long, arduous journey across the treacherous mountains, and around the endless roads to the site of his abode was filled with angst.

Then the glee of the moments spent together, and the sullen sinking rush of tears when they departed, caused further stress. An empty winter finally gave way as spring arrived. Summer seemed all too soon at an end. Blustery autumn followed; then another gloomy winter, in which the mountain passes were not travelable once again

Trula continued to teach during her terms. In the summer, young Lillie Evans would come around in the twilight hours, as the golden sun descended placidly on the western horizon. Sitting against a fencepost, she would play her bright silvery saxophone, carrying its melodious notes through the breadth of the valley, and along the shores of the river. But handsome young Rowe paid her no mind, though she desperately hoped that he might.

Trula with students Joe and Angie Kuhl
Spring Willow School, Sheridan, Wyoming,
1930-31

Chapter Eleven

"Ethel, the hateful take'd law's just not right. I've done all I can think of since I've been on the school board to get it changed. We can take care of Lansing, and we can't do it as long as he's a ward of the state."

"I agree, of course, Hon. What should we do?"

"We've got to get him back, and leave Wyoming. I wrote and told Harley about this, and he wants us to move back to Scaly. Papa's in bad health."

"I'll miss gettin' to see Addie and her kids, and I know you'll miss Wilkins, and your friends like the Yalowizors, and the Ghostbulls. But we don't see them as much nowadays, anyway. And we've gotta do what's right."

"Well, I've prayed about it, Love, and I know God will be with us."

"Now we can only take the necessary stuff. This Model A isn't going to hold all your little wants and whims." Ansel didn't look happy either.

"How about my agates, Papa?" Atlas asked.

"I've got some rocks, too. How about my books? I have a brand new set of World Book Encyclopedias, you know." Trula said.

"No to both of you on the rocks. You can take the encyclopedias, and your better books. They may be of some use."

The truck was brim full and running over on that crisp spring morning in early April, 1932. Though many items had to be abandoned, to the chagrin of the children, the engine started after only two cranks, and the trip toward North Carolina was on.

The weekend of their next visit, they had been granted their request to bring Quinn home on leave. By this time, the Vinsons had the final additions to their family: Steve, now four, and baby Phil.

"We were plannin' on willin' our ranch to you, Rowe," Mr Beaumont had said. Moisture formed in his eyes as he choked back his loneliness. "We have no family. God go with you, son. What will you do with your car?"

"I sold my Star to John Pilch. I'll miss you both very much," he had said, as he hugged the Beaumonts goodbye.

"Do you know what today is? It's your birthday, Son!" Ethel said.

"Oh, goodness! It is, isn't it!" Atlas rubbed his eyes and yawned. "April 20th! I'm ten! I can't believe it. Where are we?"

"This is Coffeyville, Kansas."

"Gee, look at that! There's dust all over the truck, and all over everything!"

"How did you kids sleep? There's been a sandstorm blowing all night. The whole area's a virtual dust bowl." Ethel's eyes were like droopy shades.

Slowly, but surely, they moved on. The next adventure lay around the bend, and over the next rise.

A sign at the crest of a ridge read "Hilltop, Unincorporated."

"What are we going to do?" Ansel asked Ethel. "The truck's out of gas, and all of the money's gone."

Arkansas proved to be a friendly place. Ansel found work within a day. The owner of a gas station needed a shed built for used tires. Others needed carpentry work done.

Their temporary home was a small room in a local motor court. Their frayed nerves soon seemed like onion skin.

"I got a letter from Harley today", Ansel announced one night. "He says Papa's getting a lot better. My half brother, Tolliver, who owns a store in Dillard, has been seeing to him. He's had good doctoring. I've got work with Tommy Gibbs in Harrison which will keep us going for a while, and he's going to provide us a place to stay, a cute little house near the Bartlett farm, just down the road a piece."

"Yay!" said Quinn.

"Hip-hip- hooray!" the others chimed in.

"Papa, I've got to get me a job. You know I can't just sit around when you're the only one working and not making much. I'll find something."

"Jobs are really tough to find, Son. I don't expect you'll find anything. I've talked to lots of older men with families who are out of work. We're in the worst depression we've ever known."

"Here, Son," Ethel said, "here's a quarter. That'll buy you some lunch. I hope you get a good job. We sure could use the money."

"Brack Tramplin's the name, what your's?"

"Rowe. Rowe Vinson. We stopped here on our way from Wyoming to North Carolina. I'm out looking for work."

"Hey! Me, too. Guess we can walk along together."

"That's fine. Boy, I'm gettin' hungry."

"Let's stop and sit on these stumps. Looks like somebody's been doin' a bunch of clearing."

"Yeah."

"My mama made me a sandwich, I'll just lay it on this stump, and we can divide it."

"No, you dang hateful mutt! That's our lunch!"

"Stinkin' dog! Hey, there's an apple tree."

"Shoot, Rowe, there ain't no apples under it, and I don't see nary a one on it neither!"

"I guess we'll just sit here and rest a spell. I've got a quarter my mama gave me. That'll get us somethin' to eat."

"Hey, there's a couple of guys over there by that house. Let's see if they know where we can find work."

The tall man looked foreboding, but the younger, dark complexioned one had a smile.

"Hey, fellas, do either of you know where we might find work?"

"How old are you boys?" the tall man asked.

"I'm nineteen," Rowe said.

"I'm eighteen."

"Sorry, boys. You have to be twenty-one to work for me. Mike," he said to the short man, "why don't you hire these boys? You could go back over the area which you've just cut. There are still plenty of small trees which could still make the grade for whisky barrel staves."

"Well," said Mike, "if I hire one of you, I'll have to hire both of you. It takes two to swing a crosscut saw. I pay seventy-five cents a day. Can you both come to my house tonight for supper? I live in Ponkey"

"Hey, man, you're on," Rowe said. Brack smiled and nodded.

Trula was soon to teach in her second school in Hilltop. It was called Willow Springs.

"You may have trouble here," she was told. "We have some pretty mischievous boys."

The girls were a pleasure, and, as usual, she had no trouble putting the boys in their place

"Leroy Bartlett has asked me to ride to church on his horse with him." Trula said one day. "He's a really nice young man."

"I see no harm in that. At least it's church, and not a honky-tonk." Ethel said.

The invitation evolved into a regular Sunday activity. Trula arose early, whistling about her choirs, and donning her most attractive dresses. After church she would accompany her suitor to dinner at his parents farm, and while away hours in carefree riding about the countryside. Those magic days carried a special charm, the first such feeling that she had ever known.

"Sis is in love!" Dan chided.

"D-don't tease her!" Quinn said, "I love my Sissy, too!"

"Pshaw! It'll happen to all of you some day!" Ansel said. "It's just the way of nature. Sure, Quinn, we all love our Sis! But she's going to find a nice fellow and settle down some day. It might even be Leroy."

But it was not to be. A girl named Charlotte came to town, and Leroy was smitten. Two years went by as surely as if it had been two days, and the Vinsons moved on. It was time to go home. And the Gibbs family, who had become so close, went along, and found a new frontier awaiting them in Carolina, as well as a young man named Oscar May.

Trula on Bartlett farm, Arkansas, 1934

Vinson children,"on the House"
At Scaly, NC, 1930's

Chapter Twelve

"I-I don't like it too much up here in Johnson Holler."

"We won't be here too much longer, Quinn. Your uncle Marshall and Aunt Callie have been really good to us, letting us stay here till I can build us a house."

The cabbage farm covered many acres in the hollow, and was the talk of the Flats Community. The Vinson boys would come in handy as workers there.

It was the summer of '34. Young Otis Burnette wheeled up in his shiny new pickup, which he had bought to haul cabbage to market.

"Hey, you fellas want a lift? Where y'all headed?"

"Hey, thanks, Ote. Rowe and I are goin' up to clean the church. They tell us that the extra folks during the revival tracked in a bunch of mud. We'll just climb in the bed," Dan said.

"Let's stay near the back, and we can hop out when we get to the church."

"Sure, sounds like fun."

"Hey, he's gettin' a little fast, Bro, hold on to that sideboard!"

"Hey! Ote!" Dan yipped. The curve had proved too sharp; the boys flew through the air to the rough road below.

"Rowe! Rowe! Are you alright? Oh, gee! What are you doing? Ote, I tried to get your attention."

"We've gotta get him out of here. He's heavin' and writhin' somethin' awful. Rowe, talk to us."

Ote carefully pushed the break pedal as he reached the Post Office.

"Uncle John, what do you think we should do?"

"This boy's worse off than you think. Get him home right away and let his parents decide what to do with him."

"Take him upstairs and lay him down on his bed," Ansel said.

"Im going up on the hill and pray," Dan said.

"Oh-h-h! What happened?"

"Hey! Papa, he's coming around. I knew he would be alright," Dan had a peaceful look on his face. He had developed a great faith which would guide him through life.

The daffodils gleamed after the soft rain's fresh bath. An early March freeze had almost extinguished their friendly glow.

Quinn

"Hand me that hammer," Ansel said to Quinn, who had bravely climbed the ladder to the top, and was peeping upward at his father. Ansel had nailed short planks on the roof as he had lain out the shake shingles. The huge two-story house was coming along rapidly, as its builder was one of the best in the country. Before he even began on it, he was getting requests from neighbors to work on their homes. Money was tight. The depression had claimed its toll on everyone.

"S-sure, Papa. Can I help you build? I can hit nails, y-you said so yourself." Quinn nodded as he spoke, his eyebrows arched.

"Not up here, Quinn," Ansel spoke sternly. And be careful going back down. You shouldn't have climbed up here."

"Aw, Papa! Y-you worry too much. I-I'm OK!"

"Just do what I say, Son, and don't argue with me."

"O-oh alright. I'm bein' careful."

"Where's Attie and Phil? How about Steve."

"A-Attie and Phil are inside with Elsie and Jesse. They all wanted to help Mama with lunch. I don't know about S-Steve."

"Wanted to eat it, if you ask me."

By this time, Quinn was on the ground. "R-Rowe an' Dan went with Oscar May. If I can't help you here, why didn't you let m-me go with them?"

"Now you know they were working with the Burnettes planting cabbage today. You would have only been in their way. Now be a good boy, and go inside with the others."

Quinn whimpered as he drifted into the yard. They were living in a small part of the house which had been completed.

"S-Steve! Wh-what are you doing back there?"

"Sh-h-h-h! Don't let Mama and Papa know where I am!" Steve choked as he blew out a large puff of smoke.

"Wh-where'd you get that p-pipe? Papa will k-kill you!"

"He won't if you don't rat on me. I'll get you if you do!"

"P-Papa! Steve's got your pipe! He's talkin' bad to me!'

"What in thunderation are you talking about? Where is Steve?"

"He's behind the outhouse s-smokin'!"

Ansel was down the ladder before he realized that he had left the roof. His mind was fixed on the matter at hand.

"Steve! You get yourself here this second!"

"Yes, Papa."

"What have you been doing? Quinn wouldn't lie to me. Where is my pipe?"

A thud on the ground answered his question. But the ground wasn't the only place that received a thud. Steve was never caught smoking again.

That afternoon when Trula arrived home from teaching in Scaly, her mother met her at the door.

"There's a sick hen out there in the coop. I told Jesse to kill it and bury it, but I haven't heard it squawk yet. Would you please get him out there?"

"Jesse, have you looked at this hen? It doesn't look that sick."

"Mama says get rid of it. We gotta do what she says. And I don't wantta eat any old sick hen, anyway."

"I'm going to talk to her. Money's still not growing on trees nowadays"

"But, Mama! Are you sure we couldn't boil it and make dumplings? Is she that sick?"

"I said get rid of it, and that's that."

"Shall we gather at the river, the beautiful, the beautiful river, gather with the saints at the river that flows by the throne of God!"

The people all raised their hands and joyously worshiped, as the pianist continued to play.

"Today we have a group of visiting singers," the preacher announced. "They are the Fox Trio from Sylva."

"Thank you, pastor. I'm Minnie, this is Nell, and Lottie. We sing for the glory of the Lord."

After church, Trula was anxious to meet the Fox sisters, as were the Kell and Anders girls.

"Hi, I'm Trula Vinson. I teach school here. We live just down the road. I already spoke to Mama, and she said you would all be welcome to come to our house for dinner. There's plenty to go around. We've got a big family of mostly boys, except for my sister, Elsie, and me."

"Hey, Minnie, hey, Nell, hey, Lettie. We all enjoyed your singing. My name's Bessie Mae Kell, and this is my sister, Annie Bell."

"It's good to meet you all."

"Don't forget us. We're the Anders sisters. I'm Dorothea, and this is Mary, Rea, Vertie, and Ruby. We live not too far from here, too."

"What about the dinner?" Trula said.

"I don't know," Minnie said. "We've got to get back to Sylva, and I don't want to slight anybody else."

"Thank you all so much," Minnie Fox said. "You folks have been more than generous. The food was scrumptious. You'll have to come to see us some time."

"You're as welcome as the flowers in springtime!" Ethel was smiling. The extra people didn't bother her. "The more the merrier, I always say."

"C-come back," said Quinn, bashfully peeping from behind the kitchen door.

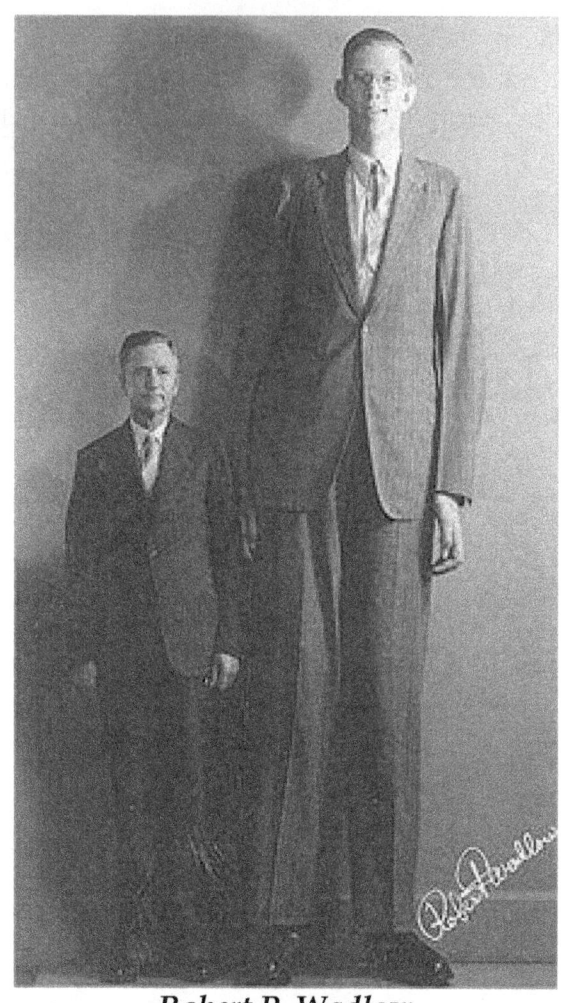

Robert P. Wadlow
Tallest man in the world,
with his father

Chapter Thirteen

"And now, ladies and gentlemen, without further ado, it gives me great pleasure to introduce the man you've all been waiting for, from Alton, Illinois, the tallest man in the world! Let's hear a big round of applause for Robert Pershing Wadlow!"

"How tall are you, Mr. Wadlow?" Rowe yelled.

"I'm over eight feet and still growing."

"W-wow!" Quinn whispered. "I-I've never seen a giant before. I-I bet he's taller than G-Goliath!"

"Pretty close, I reckon, but I've got a feeling Mr. Wadlow wouldn't hurt a flea."

"How'd you get so big?" a voice rang out in the crowd.

"My size is caused by my pituitary gland being overactive. The pituitary gland is at the base of our brain, and produces a hormone which affects our growth."

"How old are you? Ya look pretty young."

"I'm just seventeen."

"Hey, Quinn, he's your age," Dan whispered.

Clayton, Georgia was a short drive down the mountain from Scaly. It was a sunny Saturday in July, 1931. Wadlow was only on a small promotional tour before his senior year of high school. Rowe was permanently impressed, but Quinn was mesmerized.

"Come on boys, get the lead out of your britches! These cabbages aren't gonna last forever!" Marshall Brunette was a savvy businessman, and time was money. Lansing had begged to help Rowe and Dan with the July harvest.

"Quinn, just take these and lay them in the back of Ote's truck. I'll give you a quarter when we get home." Dan was patient, and loving.

"O-oh, goody! A whole two bits!"

"That's right, Quinn, maybe you can get a shave and a haircut!"

Quinn laughed so hard that Dan threatened to send him to the shade.

The summer seemed to fly, and soon, the frost lay heavy on the deep orange pumpkins. The Vinson children who were born in the West were beginning to not miss it so very much.

Rowe struck up a romance with Rea Anders. She and her family had become great friends.

"A-are you and R-Rea gonna get m-married?" Quinn asked.

"Now don't tease me, Quinn! Rea's a special girl. Only time will tell."

The Vinson family at Scaly, about 1936

Chapter Fourteen

"President Roosevelt's talking about everybody getting electric power," Trula said, "I heard them talking about it at the store on the way home from the school."

"That'll be the day," Ethel laughed.

"Quinn's going to be eighteen day after tomorrow. Let's have him a surprise party."

"Sure, why not. Have you gotten anything for him yet?"

"I bought him a pair of overalls at Drymans' the other day. Didn't I show them to you?"

"Well, if you did, I don't remember it. With all that's been going on, my mind's been in a fizz. I've been shut up in this house every day, taking care o' younguns, and with the snow, I think I've got cabin fever."

"Mama, I understand. You need to get out more. We'll get Rowe or Dan to take you for a ride and you can get Lansing a present."

"Happy birthday to you, happy birthday to you! Happy birthday dear Quinn, happy birthday to you!"

"A-aw, shucks! Y-you shouldn't have done this! But thank y'all a lot! I love you Mama, I love you P-papa. I love you S-sissy, I love you R-rowe, I l-love you E-essie, l-l..."

"We know, " Dan smiled.

"We wanted to do it," Steve said.

"Yeah," Elsie said, then Phil, and each one hugged him.

"Remember, Quinn, you're our special boy! I told you when we were still out West that we couldn't do without you for one day."

Quinn's eyes were wet. "I-I know, Papa, I know."

Quinn

"Quinn's sick Mama."

"What's wrong with him?"

"I don't know," Elsie said. "We were playin', and he just started lookin' pale, and started throwin' up."

"Where is he now?"

"Out on the porch. He's just sittin' there with his head down."

"Well, get him in here, for heaven's sake!"

"Quinn! Mama said come inside"

"I-I don't feel like it. I just wantta sit here for a b-bit."

"Quinn! Get yourself in this house this very minute. It's too cold out there, and you're sick anyway"

"I-I got my coat on. O-o-h-h! My head feels dizzy."

"Lay down here on the davenport. I'll get you some water."

"W-w-water? I don't know if I can k-keep it down. I'm just s-so sick!"

"When Papa get's home, I'll have him see about a doctor. Or maybe Rowe or Dan, if they get here first. I can't leave you, and the doctor's all the way up in Highlands."

"O-oh, Mommie! Thank you for bein' with me. I've got such a good mama!"

"Just lay still, Quinn. Do you feel like you need to throw up any more?"

"M-maybe. I d-don't know."

"Here, use this old pot if you need it."

"Ansel, I'm so glad you're home. Lansing's sick. Take a look at him. He doesn't look good. He's thrown up off and on all day."

"Son, what's wrong? How are you feeling?"

"N-not so good, Papa. I feel aw-awful."

"I'm going after Doc Wiley in Highlands. You just hang in there."

"I-I don't know, Papa. Maybe Jesus needs me like he did Eula."

"Don't say that, Son."

The winter sun rolled silently out from behind the bank of storm clouds, as if to say a new page in the Vinson saga was beginning. Rowe lowered his umbrella.

"We will never forget him. He didn't quite make nineteen, but he changed all of our lives."

"Yes, Rowe, God put him in this family as our special angel. He brought us back South. For some reason, this is where we're supposed to be."

"Yes, Papa, I really believe that." Rowe pulled Ansel to him. Old Amos laid his head between his paws, and whined softly.

"We have no marker to put on your grave, Son. But you're with God, now." Ansel closed his eyes as he tossed in a shovel-full of cold, wet dirt.

THE END

www.ingramcontent.com/pod-product-compliance
Lightning Source LLC
Chambersburg PA
CBHW031408040426
42444CB00005B/461